STEPHEN, THE FIRST MARTYR

Acts 6—7 for Children

Written by Connie Hodges
Illustrated by Betty Wind

ARCH BOOKS

Copyright © 1985 CONCORDIA PUBLISHING HOUSE

3558 S. Jefferson Avenue, St. Louis, MO 63118-3968

Manufactured in the United States of America

Though Jesus had returned to heaven
The twelve disciples still
Continued living as He said
And taught His holy will.

Soon, Jesus Christ had many friends;
Their numbers grew and grew.
The twelve disciples preached—and fed
The poor (but missed a few).

Although they tried to do it all,
They saw they were unable
To spread the Holy Word of God
And still serve every table.

"We'll choose among us seven men,
The very best we'll ask.
Men with the Holy Spirit filled
Are needed for this task."

So, all the Christians thought and prayed,
And then they chose the seven
To feed the hungry lambs of God
With food that God had given.

"Stephen should be one of them,"
The people all agreed.
"His faith is strong; he'll feed the poor
And meet their every need."

Willingly he took the task—
It made him feel so glad
That he would often preach of Christ
(Which made some people mad).

They didn't like what Stephen said
About God's saving grace;
Nor did they think that Jesus came
To save the human race.

"He cursed our God and Moses' Law,"
These evil people said;
"He says that Jesus is the Lord"—
They wanted Stephen dead.

They pulled together quite a mob
And nabbed him unaware;
Then took him to the council hall
To have him punished there.

Within the council Stephen stood,
A light around his face.
They said,
    "He speaks against the Law,
Against this holy place.

"He says that Jesus Christ has come
To change the way we pray
And take away the customs that
Have always been this way."

"No!" cried Stephen. "That's not true!
It's Moses' words I love.
He and others prophesied
Of Jesus from above.

"You got the Law direct from God
But didn't hold it dear.
And now you've killed the Righteous One!"
Said Stephen loud and clear.

They hated what he said to them;
Their anger filled the air.
But Stephen fell upon his knees
And looked to God in prayer.
The Holy Spirit filled his eyes;
He was overawed.
"Behold! I see the Son of Man!
He's standing next to God!"

The council shouted, "Blasphemy!"
And dragged him out of town.
And, just beyond the city gates,
They stoned him to the ground.

Aware that death was now at hand,
Stephen didn't fear it.
Instead, he prayed to God these words:
"Lord Jesus, take my spirit.

"Please, forgive this sin of theirs,
Though it be wide and deep."
Then Stephen—faith-filled servant—fell
Into eternal sleep.

DEAR PARENTS:

Stephen was the first Christian martyr. Probably a Greek-speaking Jew, it is likely that Stephen came from abroad to live in Jerusalem. Like Philip (probably also another Hellenistic Jew [Acts 6:8]), Stephen was to have an effect on the church far beyond the duties for which he had been appointed originally.

Of all the members of the Jerusalem church, Stephen especially seems to have had a clear understanding of the ultimate break with Old Testament worship practices that commitment to the new faith involved. And it was his exceptional grasp of this fact that so enraged his accusers and the Sanhedrin: "they covered their ears and, yelling at the top of their voices, they all rushed at him, dragged him out of the city and began to stone him" (Acts 7:57-58 NIV).

Stephen's death marked the beginning of a more general persecution of the Jerusalem church. In the end, however, this persecution and the scattering of the believers at Jerusalem that followed did more good than harm, because they carried the Good News with them, acting in a way as forerunners of Paul and others.

The murder of an innocent man by a mob is a tragedy of the first degree. But even in Stephen's death we can see the hand of God working for good: "those who had been scattered preached the word wherever they went" (Acts 8:4 NIV).

As you talk with your child about Stephen's death, explain that we call the death of a Christian "sleep" because we believe Jesus' promise that those who trust in Him as their Savior live with Him in heaven forever.

THE EDITOR